What people are saying about *Living Intentionally: How to Bring Balance to You and Your Family*

Living with intention is living with personal power to accomplish your highest aspirations and goals. But how do you know that you are truly living with intention? What does it look like? What does it feel like? There are moments of activity in our life that are certainly driven by intention, but how do we harness the Energy of Intention to guide us to do more, serve more and be more? Amy Smalarz and her Intentional Living crusade has me asking these questions on a daily basis. She haunts me with these questions . . . but in a loving and supportive way. Imagine being the person of your dreams, living the life of your dreams and knowing exactly what you should be doing as you move through your life. Living with intention is living with ultimate freedom. Amy Smalarz is my tour guide for Intentional living.

> ~ Jeff Moore, President - International Pacific Seafoods, LLC / Founder Thursday Night Boardroom Global Mastermind / Co-Host - The Deep Dive Podcast

Amy delivers a clear path to truly Living Intentionally, and this book will help you identify, define, and live your life with intention. She captivates your attention from the first chapter and keeps you glued until the end. This book will be a keeper in your library, and I highly recommend it.

> ~ Christopher Cumby, Author, The Success Playbook

The idea of living with intention has a long legacy. From the immortal Dr. Wayne Dyer to the transformational Robin Sharma, great leaders have aspired to help humanity understand the power of living intentionally, and its ability to change lives for the better. No one knows this better than Amy Smalarz. Amy understands that intention cannot be isolated to any one aspect of your life, but must be consistent and congruent across all aspects. Her perspectives are much needed in this world, and I'm excited to watch her make this tremendous contribution.

> ~ Alex Charfen, Co-founder and CEO of CHARFEN, Author of "Entrepreneurial Personality Type: Your guide to the most important and misunderstood people among us"

Work-Life Balance is a myth. You can't possibly feel balanced when you're living in a reaction-based world—constantly driven by the next task or person who needs something from you. So, instead of letting life just happen to you, Smalarz suggests a different path. *Living Intentionally* shows you how to create momentum in your life by thoughtfully setting the direction you want to move. If you're stressed out and fed up—this book can help.

> ~ Julie Anne Eason, author of *The Work at Home Success Guide* and *The Profitable Business Author*

LIVING INTENTIONALLY:

How to Bring Balance to You and Your Family

www.warriorpublishinghouse.com or www.amysmalarz.com

Library of Congress Control Number: 2016913132

ISBN: 978-0-9978671-0-7

Printed in the United States of America

Ordering Information:
Quantity sales. Special discounts are available on quantity purchases by coaches, teams, associations, and others. For details, contact the publisher at the address above, or by email: amy@amysmalarz.com.

Dedication

To my boys: my husband and soul mate, Davey, and my two sons, Matty and Benny:
I love you and how you put up with my craziness, always endure my spirit, and
allow me to shine! And even though I wrote this in 2015, they are words that will
last a lifetime.

Seeing your smile and feeling your touch,
Your warmth, your love, fills me with joy.
Watching you come into your own,
Challenge yourself and being
Confident enough to try . . .
Causes me to stop, take a breath and smile.
I feel my eyes bring with tears of love. awe and joy.
You represent what I strive to be and you
Amaze me every day.
Your gentle soul and your determined heart and mind
Are a blessing to me and a wonderful gift to the world.
May you always be free to love, care for and respect others.
May you always be free to try, explore and test your limits.
May you be free to find love and share your true selves . . . for
Your gentle soul and determined heart and mind
Will be your beacon, your light, your LIFE.

Love,
Mama

Table of Contents

Author's Note

I recently had a phone conversation with a friend and mentor and he asked me a few questions that are relevant to *Living Intentionally: How to Bring Balance to You and Your Family*:

> "What does it mean to live a life of intention?"

> "What does it look and feel like?"

And he was just getting warmed up!

These may be questions you have as you begin to read this book – and like him, you are probably just getting warmed up, too. And while these questions will be answered, I encourage you to take your time and be easy on yourself. You are giving yourself a great gift right now. You recognize that while you are busy doing a lot of 'things' you are not as focused or as deliberate or as *Intentional* as you want to be.

When talking about Intention, I like to think of it as my Life's Journey. I have spent years on this road learning through my ups and downs – and I wrote this book to help you shorten your own learning curve.

I also wrote this book because often times the words "Purpose" and "Intention" are used interchangeably but they are not the same. I like to think of it this way:

> Your *purpose* is your WHY, the reason for which something is done or created or for which something exists;

> Your *intention* is your aim, your plan, your blueprint for achieving it.

Living Intentionally: How to Bring Balance to You and Your Family, shows you how to build your own Home, creating a space for YOU, where you can be your best, truest self. And it all starts with you. I know that in today's society, that is a bit counterintuitive because you may feel that doing something for yourself is being selfish. But let me ask you, if you don't spend time on you, with yourself, how can you bring your best self to others?

Now, I fully admit that I'm not perfect (my husband, family and friends can attest to that) but I am committed to this Living Intentionally Movement! You have made of leap of faith with me and that is not something I take lightly. I'm so honored and excited that you are a part of it with me.

Amy Smalarz, 2016

Foreword

I didn't know I needed this book until I read it.

As an entrepreneur, I'm fortunate to live a life that brings new joys (and obstacles) every day. Over the years my brother Matthew and I have enjoyed starting and optimizing a variety of businesses, including a premium pet food company, a bar and restaurant, multiple magazines, and several online communities including YoungEntrepreneur.com, BizWarriors.com and Kidpreneurs.org. But even with that level of variety, I, too have fallen into the "survive, not thrive" mindset Amy Smalarz describes in her book, *Living Intentionally: How to Bring Balance to You and Your Family.*

When the going gets tough and there's too much to juggle at once, it's easy to slip into autopilot. Once that happens—once our circumstances are dictated for us, as Amy puts it—we lose the ability to live intentionally, to look back at the end of the day with appreciation and pride. It doesn't even matter what we do each day. It's how and why we do things that change how we view our own lives. Whether you're an entrepreneur, a doctor, an artist, a stay-at-home parent, or even a student, you've likely experienced this mindset before. No matter what, you're not alone—and there is a solution.

When I met Amy, I could see right away that her purpose is to help others get to a place where they are living their best lives. *Living Intentionally* is a book that will do just that!

Between these pages, there are simple (yet effective) strategies to help you make choices that improve your life, in areas both personal and professional. Amy's lessons, or balancing acts, guide you through the seamless process of transforming your mindset into something more positive and productive. Instead of barely surviving each week, you'll shift to being able to thrive.

Amy is a lifelong student with a thirst for learning that can't be quenched. Even with a Ph.D. in Social Policy, Health Services Research, and Health Economics, Amy picks the minds of her mentors to build upon her knowledge. Her experience as an entrepreneur and Certified High Performance Coach breaks through her lessons to help others build healthy, happy, and sustainable lives while maintaining their professional ones. "Living Intentionally," Amy's podcast, offers a wealth of Amy's secrets on living with intention each and every day. Amy has even brought so much focused positivity to her own family that her little ones, Matty and Benny, are working on starting their own ninja warrior course business! Her dedication to learning, rich personal experience, and can-do attitude blend to make Amy the perfect coach.

I found Amy's book, *Living Intentionally: How to Bring Balance to You and Your Family*, to be both enjoyable and practical. Her straightforward, no-fluff-included balancing acts help us focus our energy to create less stressful lives. Best of all, Amy's charming demeanor guides you through the process of living intentionally at the perfect pace. There's no pressure to complete the process before you're ready—but your own excitement should make the steps relatively quick.

Living Intentionally helped me thrive day-to-day, and I hope it will do the same for you.

Adam Toren
Award winning Author, Entrepreneur, Digital Marketer, Advisor & Life Enthusiast

Introduction

Why do you need more balance in your life?

"Time and balance are the two most difficult things to have control over, yet they are both the things that we do control." –Catherine Pulsifer

When you woke up today, how did you feel? Were you excited and eager to get going? Or were you like many other people: preparing for the same thing, just on a different day?

Are you surviving or thriving?

Are your circumstances being dictated to you, or are you choosing to live Intentionally?

This is not to say that you don't have fun at times, but more frequently there are days when the daily grind and stress get to you. There are so many things to juggle at once: dealing with nonsense at work, trying to figure out what's important to take care of first, then struggling with the inevitable guilt about focusing on that one thing.

Are you just wishing there was *one more hour* in the day?

We try to pack so many things in our day that we simply don't have the chance to sit and relax.

Now, just reading those words, I can see your head shaking or eyes rolling. You might even have said:

"Ha! **Sit back and relax**?! Who is this crazy lady that says I should have time to sit and relax?"

But let me ask you a question. Does the following situation sound at all familiar?

It's Friday night, and you are finally lying on the couch after a long week (and maybe even longer night.) The kids are in bed or out with friends, and there is some quiet.

When you think back on the week, do you feel fulfilled? Do you smile and say, "Wow! This week was awesome," or do you think to yourself, "Well, looks like we survived another one . . ."

Before you know it, you start to go through the agenda for the weekend: sports practices or games, music lessons, play dates, errands, chores, and so on. Then you skip right up to Monday, knowing you are going to do it all over again. So before you even give yourself a few moments to relax and enjoy your Friday night, you are already tired, stressed, overwhelmed, and maybe even anxious about all of the things you have coming your way. Again comes the monotony and overload.

The illusion of work-life balance is still out there, and the way some people talk about it, it sounds like low-hanging fruit. You think:

if I can just get this schedule a bit tighter,

if I didn't have to deal with some of the nonsense at work,

· *if* I could just be better with my time,

if I could be more productive,

if I could get up earlier and stay up later,

then I would have more work-life balance.

But all of this is a trap because there is no work-life balance.

We beat ourselves up in hopes of achieving this elusive balance, when in reality, it doesn't exist. There is just balancing LIFE and what you have in front of you.

Having Intention is having direction!

You feel like you are failing—in life, with your family, with your friends, at work and within yourself. You are constantly spinning your wheels or at a standstill, with no true direction.

But:

Imagine waking up in the morning and giving yourself a few minutes to set your actions for the day.

Imagine knowing the direction you want to be heading, then setting your agenda based on what is important for you versus urgent for others.

Imagine making decisions based on whether they are growth opportunities for you, helping you to move toward your positive direction, or if they are depleting ones that will take you away from the direction you want to be headed.

Imagine sitting on your couch on Friday nights and smiling about what you did during the week. Not only what you gave yourself, but what you contributed, how you made decisions, and how you took action to keep moving forward.

By the time you finish reading this book, you will have the tools and roadmap you need to take back control of your LIFE!

No more wishing you had one more hour in the day.

No more wondering where the days or weeks have gone.

No more looking for the latest technology or app to help you optimize your schedule or to-do list.

You will know exactly how to set your own direction with Intention, and work toward following it each and every day. That is what living Intentionally means.

The Merriam-Webster Dictionary defines "intention" this way:

in·ten·tion

in ˈten(t)SH(ə)n/

noun

1. a thing intended; an aim or plan.

At the end of this book, you will have your own, personalized definition of what Living Intentionally means to you.

You will get your time back because, not only will you be engaged in projects you want to be a part of, but you will also have the tools for saying 'no' to things that don't bring you joy or fulfillment.

Gone are the days when you wake up dreading what's ahead.

Gone are the days in which you feel as though you made it through by the skin of your teeth.

Gone are the days of just getting by.

Here are the days of Living Intentionally: setting your own direction with Intention, and following it each and every day.

Chapter 1

When was your New First Day?

> *"Today is the first day of the rest of your life."*
> Abbie Hoffman, *Revolution for the Hell of It*

It was a Tuesday afternoon in May of 2013. As I was getting ready to close my laptop for the afternoon, make my mad dash to the express train, and get home in time to pick up the boys from daycare, one last email came through. It literally stopped me in my tracks.

It was a meeting request for the next morning. Meeting invites is not so unusual, but the tone and implied urgency raised some red flags for me. So much so that I immediately called my mentor at the time and asked if she could meet me for coffee the next morning. In my gut, I knew something was up, but I just wasn't sure *what*.

The next morning, at 6:30 AM, Margaret said to me:

> *"Amy, you don't have a poker face—you just weren't born with one, and people can read you like a book. So use what you do have to your advantage. Sit quietly, observe and listen—you are good at that. Whatever the news, don't show shock or disappointment or surprise. Expect the unexpected, and you will be prepared."*

As it turns out, it was the best advice she could have given me. When I arrived at work and walked into the boardroom, everyone was there—except our President, as he had been let go the night before. None of us saw it coming, not this fast, not this way.

As if this wasn't enough, the person who was given the temporary position to run the US office was someone for whom I knew I could never work. We had never seen eye-to-eye, and let's just say I didn't appreciate his mode of office politics.

I was devastated. Not only to lose a boss I looked up to and respected—I had just left a job 18 months before to come work for the now-fired boss. Not to mention my team was just getting into a groove . . . and then this happened. I had a scared, empty feeling of ,"Oh shit, now what?"

Have you ever had this feeling? Of knowing you need to leave or change, but you don't know which direction to take?

I knew in my head and my gut that I couldn't stay there. But where to go? The idea of going through another job search and probably ending up in the same rat race wasn't appealing. I felt stuck, afraid and frankly a bit useless as I was realizing that this just wasn't for me.

But if not this . . . then what?

At this moment, many things came flooding to my mind. And there is one in particular that I would like to share with you now.

When I was a little girl, I had a couple of surgeries in hospitals but I was not the ordinary patient. I loved the sights, the sounds, even the *smells*! I would ask the surgeon if I could see what he was taking out of me or if he could videotape the procedure. And as I grew up, I knew I wanted to help people be well, be strong. So naturally, I thought I would become a pediatric surgeon because they had helped me be well and strong. But my C+ in organic chemistry put the kibosh on that. However, I found mentors like Professor Gordie and Alice and Nancy and Torch along the way who showed me that I could help people without having to be a surgeon. So, after graduating Brandeis University with degrees in Biology and Sociology, gaining experience in the health insurance industry, I moved my way up the ladder while earning a master's degree, then my Ph.D.. All the while, I was following the path I figured I was supposed to take, or what I thought was expected of me. I was deemed successful: always moving up, taking on new roles and responsibilities. Yet I never felt I was living up to my potential. But throw a husband, house, dog, and kids into the mix, and after a while, it got easy to stop questioning my own fulfillment and instead focus on "getting things done."

Now, granted, no one told me I had to take this path, but there are signals that seem to say certain paths are "good" or "right" or "proper." The problem was, many of the jobs I had done left me with a feeling of dissatisfaction. I tried to get rid of that feeling by changing roles, switching departments, and even changing companies.

Back in May 2013 it was time to make a decision: stay with the organization, or do something else.

It took me a couple days to figure it out, but once I did, it hit me like a ton of bricks. I had been on cruise control for **years**! I had been doing what I *thought* I was supposed to do: go to college, get multiple degrees, work my way up the ladder, work lots of hours and sacrifice myself—all of it. I felt as though I was either spinning my wheels or running a hundred miles an hour but going nowhere. But I never really took time to assess what I wanted from each day: what I wanted to contribute; the direction I wanted to go.

That is no way to live. I didn't want to just survive anymore. I wanted to find my direction and live each day with Intention!

This was my New First Day.

Your Journey

Problems like trying to fit everything in and be what we think others expect us to be are self-made. We have been trained, and over time, bought into this system of belief. That's what successful people do, right? Put in the time as others have done before us.

This reminds me of a scene at a local Boston hospital I observed one summer after my freshman year in college, when I was volunteering on the Surgical Intensive Care Unit (SICU). (I hadn't gotten the C+ in organic chemistry yet, so I still had my dream of being a pediatric surgeon.) As you know, doctors have to work long shifts, and when doctors are training or in residency, the other surgeons like to mess with them.. I remember asking one of the surgeons why they did this and his response was:

"It was done to me. It's just the way it's gotta be."

Now, while some of you may be appalled or upset, think about how *you* treat someone who is new to a job. Even though you may not say it, you are probably thinking, "If I had to suffer through it, so do you. It's just par for the course."

And if so, you are not alone.

Life is a puzzle, and we piece it together as we go along. Eventually the pieces are all in place. If you take one piece out, even just to replace it, that often means the entire puzzle doesn't work. That is the fear: that it will all fall apart.

This book is about your journey. This book gives you permission to stop, take a breath and ask: *Where am I going? What is my direction?* After you finish reading this book, you will know exactly how to set your own direction and how to work toward it each and every day.

Once you set your own direction and intentions, you will never want to go back. A giant weight will be lifted off your shoulders. And the crazy (or scary) part is, you may not have even realized that the weight was there—that is, until it's gone. You will stand up a little straighter. People will sense your level of self-love, self-respect and say, "**I'll have what she's having.**" You will wonder how it is that you stayed on the same path for so long.

But, at the same time, you may be wondering if any of this is possible for *you*.

Myth-Busting Time

Now, I know you may be thinking that this sounds good in theory, but there's no way to actually do this. You may even be thinking, "Yes! I totally want to do this!" but the next moment, you start thinking about all of the things you have on your plate. And the next thing you know, you are telling yourself that you don't have time to do this!

Myth #1: You don't have time to do this.
I'm here to say that you DO have time. Saying you don't have time is an excuse, and it just isn't true. And here's why.

You make time to think and possibly even worry about all of your to-do's, all of your "have-to's" every day. One of the biggest tricks I share with clients (and with you in this book) is how to replace that time with your time of Intention. In the end, you aren't taking up extra time– and after going through this process, you will most likely *gain* some of your time back!

Myth #2: Living with Intention is hard!
I hear this a lot. But take a moment to think about how you feel about your life right now. Not about the material things you have, like a car, house or job, but how you

feel when you wake up in the morning, on your way to work, driving the kids to practice, and at night when you finally have a moment to rest.

Do you feel fulfilled?

Do you feel energized?

Do you experience enjoyment?

Do you feel dread?

When you Live with Intention, you may still have your to-do list, but chances are the items on the list and the feeling you have while doing them changes completely. You no longer feel as if you "made it through the day." You are no longer just surviving.

So, I ask, which is harder: going through your days with a lack of fulfillment and enjoyment, or seeing yourself and your life in a new light—and Living in that light every day?

Having said all of this, there is plenty of bad advice out there these days.

Download this app to get more organized!

Use the latest productivity planner to get more time out of your day!

Hire one more person to take planning off your plate!

Color code your calendar!

Does any of this sound familiar? This brings me to myth #3.

Myth #3: Reorganizing the same old stuff, just in a new way, will be enough to fix your problems

I'm not saying these items are not useful. But are you looking to be innovative, or to organize the same old stuff in a "new" way?

I use technology to help organize and schedule coaching calls, podcast interviews, webinars, and other to-do's. I write in my journal every day to organize my thoughts and plan for the day, the week and the year. I'm not saying these approaches aren't helpful. But they are only helpful if you are thoughtful about where you want to be going. Reorganizing the same stuff keeps you in circles, even when it looks pretty or neat.

I know you're busy, but you've given yourself time to read this book, and you've made it this far. You *want* to bring change to your life. You are done just making it through the day, the week. You no longer want to just survive. And you want to help others in the same way. Which brings me to myth #4 . . . .

Myth #4: You have to help others before helping yourself.

Now that we have talked about you, let's talk about your family. You love them and want the best for them. You sacrifice your time, energy and money for them. But right now, you need to take care of YOU first, *before* helping them.

I have two young boys, ages 7 and 9, and they are the lights of my life! I constantly worry about whether they are eating enough, getting enough exercise, reading enough, exploring, enjoying down time, staying curious . . . Most importantly, are they being good human beings?

I am constantly asking myself if I am doing *enough* for them.

Does that sound familiar?

Do you want your children to feel the same way about life as you do, or do you want them to have a more positive and abundant mindset?

Do you want them to trudge through their weeks, or do you want them to thrive each day and wake up excited for what the day brings?

My boys wake up every morning excited for the day. They want to play, build a new village on Minecraft, design a new Ultimate American Ninja Warrior course, draw and plan out "the best video game ever"–and all before lunchtime!

And I'm not alone. I'm guessing if you have kids that many of them are the same way. They use their imaginations, are constantly looking forward to the day, and are excited about what may come their way.

But as we get older, we lose our imaginations. We don't stay curious and more often than not, we accept things "as they are."

If you stop and think about it, your kids see that. What message is that sending them? They look up to you. You are their hero, their role model. Even if you have teenagers, they emulate and model your behavior. You set the norms in their world, and if the norm is hating your job and going anyway, what do you think they will grow up to do?

I know this may sound harsh, and I even hear some "How dare you's," but it's true. Children are beautiful, bright, intelligent, curious and loving. They live each day with their eyes, ears and hearts wide open.

Why not set an example for your children and for your family of enjoying what you do? Of bringing your truest, best self in all that you do? Don't you want your children to:

> Keep that joy in the morning
> Keep that wonder
> Be open and curious?

That is why we start with YOU.

> You set the example.

You are the captain of the ship, and you need to take time to set its course. You set the pace and the tone.

It all starts with you.

I have been honored to have some amazing guests on my podcast, "Living Intentionally with Amy Smalarz," and during the writing of this book, Wesley Chapman, Founder of The Human Project, said something that really struck me:

> "Change itself isn't hard, but thinking about change and being honest with ourselves is. We have to stop lying to ourselves, which comes in the form of excuses and, face ourselves, our honest truth. Once we commit to the change, then the act of change is easy, because we are going toward our natural selves."

One line especially is worth repeating:

"The act of change is easy, because we are going toward our natural selves."

This is your life's work. It's fun, it's hard, it's amazing and you will never be the same.

How to use this book

In *Living Intentionally: How to Bring Balance to You and Your Family*, I bring you back to the basics. We start from the ground up, of taking time out to look at and into yourself. Before you can run, you need to walk, and before you walk, you need to know which direction you want to be heading. And that's where we start: your foundation. Once you are clear on your direction, you are ready to tackle the work

30

of re-thinking your important versus their urgent, your support, and defining what Living Intentionally means to you.

While you may be tempted to jump around, I strongly recommend reading this book from start to finish. The chapters build on one another, so in order to get the most out of this book, you need to follow them in order.

The Intention of this book is to help you build your "Home." And a Home consists of:

Your foundation

Your support

Your protection.

We will cover each of these in depth. And because I'm a life-long learner and teacher at heart, there is a workbook for you to download and use while reading this book. Just download the workbook from the resources page on http://amysmalarz.com/book/ and by the time you are finished with this book, you will have the blueprint for your Home.

All of the case studies and personal or client stories in this book are real. Due to non-disclosure agreements, some names have been changed. And while I cannot guarantee that you will achieve the same results as those shared in this book, if you do the work and put in the time and effort, you will be well on your way to Living Intentionally!

Ready, Set, Go!

Okay, it's time! Are you ready? By the time you finish this book, you will have a new lens, a new outlook on life. You will have done an amazing thing: given yourself time to get to know YOU, where YOU want to be going, and how YOU want to get there!

Awesome stuff, huh?

I would like to thank you for raising your hand, buying this book, and investing in yourself. I am humbled and honored to be on this journey with you. Without further ado, go ahead and turn the page and take the steps YOU need to live your life with greater Intention!

YOUR HOME

"The ache for home lives in all of us, the safe place where we can go as we are and not be questioned." –Maya Angelou

"It takes hands to build a house, but only hearts can build a home." –Unknown

"I'm not meant to live alone. Turn this house into a home."
--Luther Vandross, *A House Is Not a Home*

Chapter 2

What's the difference between a house and a Home?

As I alluded to in the previous chapter, the key to Living Intentionally is to become the architect of your own Home.'

Now before I go any further, I want to define what a Home means to me.

You may have heard the expression, "Home is where the heart is." And while I think that's true, a Home is more than just that. A Home is where you live. It's the space you choose to share with others. We all need a place to call Home, where we know we can go to be loved, respected, protected and sheltered. And putting all of this together, I refer to this process as building your Home because it involves creating a space for YOU, where you can be your best, truest self.

Now, a house is different. A house can be cold, hard and uninviting. A house is a place to stay, but it's not made for you. It doesn't reflect your personality, your style.

Doormats say "Welcome Home" not "Welcome House" for a reason.

Whether you know it or not, you have already built a structure for yourself. But chances are, it's more of a house, not a Home. It doesn't always reflect the true

YOU or how you know you want to be, what you want to contribute, or how you want to make others feel.

There are TV shows dedicated to building Homes, and my boys and I like to watch them on HGTV. "Property Brothers," "Fixer Upper" and "Love It or List It" are three of our favorites. And while each of these shows is unique and have their own style and presentation, there are some steps they follow:

- Break down the structure of the house to see what it's made of
- Design it for the people who will be living there so it reflects them, their style, their personality
- Rebuild it.

And whether it's Joanna, Jonathan or Hilary, the transformations are always amazing. They take a house, often times down to the studs, and rebuild it in the shape and style of the homeowners. They take time with the homeowners to ask questions and go through designs to ensure that their personalities shine through. Some things work and others don't. They always encounter an unexpected challenge, like mold or leaky plumbing. Yet they work through the problems, persevere and don't quit.

And at the end of the show, it never fails that each homeowner tears up when they walk into their new Home for the first time. Their Home is more than they ever dreamed it could be. It "feels like home."

And by the end of this book, you will feel the same way about yourself. You will see yourself in a new light, through a new lens.

But in order for these transformations to happen, you need to do some construction, some renovations. You will need to break the old house apart, fix the *foundation*, rebuild walls and beams for **support**, and reinforce the roof for proper *protection* so what you build will last.

And that, my friend, is what we are going to do here! You are going to design and build your Home.

Now, I realize you may not be an expert in construction or interior design. But you *are* an expert in YOU. The problem is, you probably haven't taken time to get to know YOU lately. What you want, what you are made of . . . .

And that's what we are going to do here. The process of building your Home includes three phases:

- ❖ Your foundation
- ❖ Your support
- ❖ Your protection

Too often, we don't take time to develop our own selves, the way we want to really be. We do things we think others expect of us, and we do things because we think they need to be done. I call that living in a house.

But when you follow this simple framework of building your Home:

- ❖ Your foundation
- ❖ Your support
- ❖ Your protection

Your imprint is all over it. It is fully reflective of who you are, who you want to become, and how you want to show up in the world!

Having said this, I'm guessing you have some questions in your mind, such as:

"Why not just use the house I have?"
"Do I really need to rebuild?"

The short answer is yes, you need to do some work, some renovations, some updating. While on the surface it may seem easier to just do some minor touch-ups or hide some things with a quick coat of paint, in the long run, it usually doesn't serve you well.

Have you ever been on vacation and rented a condo or house to stay for a few days? Ever notice the feeling when you walk in? You know, instinctively, that this place isn't yours, but it's nice enough. There are couches, tables, chairs, appliances. And ever notice that things seem out of place (you don't know where to find the cups or silverware)? It was designed by someone else, without you in mind. But it's a house. And you aren't staying there for too long, so you live with it as it is. You adjust and function within the house's boundaries because you know that it's temporary.

Yet many of you are living in a house like this every day. Let me ask you, do you sometimes feel out of place? Do you feel like you are living a life that was designed by someone else and you are just trying to fit in?

My guess is, if you are still reading, this resonates with you. You can take control of your house and turn it into your Home.

I can remember when my family and I moved into our house eight years ago. Sticky kitchen cabinets, weird stains on the kitchen ceiling, a big wall with a small opening between the kitchen and living room—not to mention a ridiculously big wood stove in our downstairs room that was placed almost in the middle of the space! Not ideal moving-in condition. Oh, and did I mention that a week into living there, we found out that the electrical box was melting?

It was a house and not our Home. It took many years for it to become our Home. My husband and I tackled the kitchen and those sticky cabinets and weird ceiling stains ourselves—and with the help of family and friends —when our boys were both under the age of three. That was a learning experience, for sure. I learned that leveling cabinets is *hard*, the floor is almost never level, and that you can quickly adjust to new things. I remember that it took time for me to re-adjust back to having a functional kitchen. Our renovation took about three months, and during that time I quickly adjusted to going to the bedroom to use the microwave, since that was one of the only sockets in the house wired to handle the voltage. But once the kitchen was completed, it took me about a month to remember that the microwave was actually in the kitchen and not in the bedroom. It took time for me to adjust on both ends of the spectrum. But the main lesson? I adjusted.

We have spent the last seven years renovating the rest of the house: laying new wood floors, taking down walls, putting walls up, making rooms more functional, getting rid of that awful wood stove. We have taken the time to turn what was a house into our Home.

When you are finished reading this book and have completed each of the balancing acts—fun challenges in each chapter that will help you design and build your Home along the way—you will turn your own house into your Home.

What are YOU building?

Remember, building your Home consists of three phases:

- ❖ Your foundation
- ❖ Your support

- ❖ Your protection

We start with your foundation, which consists of two parts:
- ❖ Your Guiding Words
- ❖ Your action Words of Today (WOT)

In this case, your Guiding Words are part of your foundation because they set your direction: the person you want to become, what you want to do, where you want to go. Next comes your action Words of Today (WOT), which are daily reminders of how you want to transform your Intentions or Guiding Words into your daily practice. Often times, you have anywhere from one to three action WOT each day, depending on what you would like to accomplish.

And just like a house you build with wood and other materials, if your foundation is weak, the house is bound to fall in on itself someday. It's important to take time (and we will) on understanding how you build your foundation and how you can maintain it each and every day.

Next comes your support: your walls. This is where your "important" versus their "urgent" and using your Decision Tree come in. You will have taken the time to develop a solid foundation—you know where you want to go in life, and you have your guiding words and action WOT to get you there. Now you need the daily support that frames and shapes your Home. You want to live in a Home that is filled with things that are more important to you, not everyone else's "urgent." You want a Home that is filled and maybe even overflowing with growth, not depletion and decay.

That is where the two support systems come in handy:

- ❖ Your "important" versus their "urgent"
- ❖ Your Decision Tree

We will take time for you to think about, work on and develop your support systems.

Lastly, there is your protection, the roof, the last piece that seals your home together, that protects you from too much sunlight and shields you from the rain. This is your definition of Living Intentionally. This is where the foundation and support systems are joined together to complete you, your Home.

This is the last phase because the size and shape of your roof are dependent upon your foundation and support. Your definition of Living Intentionally will not only reflect your foundation but what you use to support yourself. And as builders will tell you, while the structure of many roofs are the same, there are intricate details that are specific to each one. These are the details that if ignored, will result in that leaky roof or a space where others can invade. (Just ask my neighbor, who had a bird's nest and squirrels in hers . . . .) Just like your foundation and your support, your protection needs to be reflective of you and encompass all that you are and who you want to be. And for those of you who are parents, this changes how you are seen as a role model and example for others, especially your children.

I know I went through these quickly, but we are going to jump right into thinking about and developing your foundation. It's one thing to read about it, but it's a whole other thing entirely to start working on it for yourself.

Remember, this is meant to be an action-oriented book, so I suggest working along with the chapters. Don't forget the online resources I have made available for you with this book. Download your workbook here: http://amysmalarz.com/book/. The video library explains each of the three phases and the ideas and work behind each one.

So, without further ado, let's get working on your foundation!

Phase I:

Your Foundation

"The loftier the building, the deeper must the foundation be laid." –Thomas a Kempis

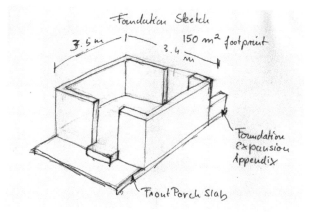

Chapter 3

What is your foundation?

One of my favorite definitions of a foundation is:

> *"an underlying basis or principle for something . . ."*

Like any good builder knows, you must start with a solid foundation when building a house. You need something sturdy that can hold the weight and support your walls, beams and roof. And this, building your own Home, is no different.

Underlying basis or principle for something . . . What is your underlying basis? What are your principles of life? How do you live those each day?

Although it may seem obvious to builders or architects, I am often asked:

> *"Amy, why do I need to start with my foundation? Why can't I jump in and set my definition of Living Intentionally?"*

Why your foundation first?

Before I answer that, take a moment to think back to the most recent goal you set for yourself. It can be large or small:

❖ I will meditate for five minutes every day

- ❖ I will stop using Splenda in my coffee
- ❖ I will put my phone away when I get home
- ❖ I will prepare better for my meetings
- ❖ I will update my resume
- ❖ I will reach 10,000 steps per day

Anything, just think of something.

Now, how well did you do with your goal?

- ❖ Did you follow through?
- ❖ Did you incorporate it into your daily life, your daily activities?
- ❖ Did you *enjoy* doing it?

If you are like 95 percent of my clients (and most people), you will either be shaking your head or thinking of reasons why you weren't able to do it. Am I right?

You know why most people have trouble following through with their goals? It's because most of you do not take time to think:

- ❖ Why is this goal important to me?
- ❖ Why now?
- ❖ Is this something I want to do for myself, or did someone else suggest it?
- ❖ On a scale of 1-10 [1 = not important at all; 10 = super important], how important is your goal to *you*?

I realize that you may have asked one or two of these questions, but most people don't ask any at all. Many people will put a goal down because it sounds good, but they don't really know WHY . . . .

And then there's the WHAT. What effort will it take from you to achieve your goal? What support will you need from others to keep you on track and help you with your goal? This is another big one that's overlooked. We, as humans, are communal creatures. We need a community or tribe—and we need support. Even if you did think about what you would need to do or change to accomplish your goal, did you take time to think about what you would need from others to help you along on your journey?

And then there is the HOW. How will you celebrate your small wins along the way? How will you keep yourself on track and remind yourself that you are making strides, and not give up on yourself or your goal?

WHY...WHAT...HOW?

[In case you are interested in learning how you can set your goals in a way that will lead to greater success, check out my online course, "3 Steps to Goal Success." You can find it on my website, amysmalarz.com, or on the resources page for this book, http://amysmalarz.com/book/. Just type in the code Success2016 to get FREE lifetime access.]

What does setting goals have to do with Living Intentionally? Well, an obvious answer is that if you are going to Live Intentionally, you need to have a path for doing so. Part of that path may involve setting specific goals.

Another reason is that many of you have experience with setting goals. Some work, others don't. And chances are, you are more successful when the goal has real meaning to you. The same goes for Living Intentionally. It's a thoughtful process, and it takes time.

Why do you want to live that way?

What will you bring out of yourself?

How will you give more of your true self to others?

Finding your direction, your purpose

We all get sidetracked. Even when we have the best intentions, we can get sidetracked. And honestly, if you say this never happens to you, A) you are lying, or B) please call me! Because I would like to know how you do it.

Seriously, though, as my coach and mentor Bo Eason says:

"We are off-course 99 percent of the time."

It's up to you to right the ship. It's your job to continually and consistently find your way back.

And that's where this comes full circle (just in case you were wondering why I threw this "goal setting stuff" in here).

How do you not just find your way back, but truly *find your way*?

It's your foundation.

If you want to build a Home that can battle storms, then you need—no, you must—start with a solid foundation: an understanding of who you are and who you want to be. And let's be clear, this goes beyond to-do lists or organizing your calendars. There are tons of great resources available for you to do that (and I use some myself), but before you can organize and prioritize, you need to know WHAT matters to you.

In the next two chapters, I introduce and walk you through how to think about and define your:

❖ Guiding Words
❖ Action Words of Today [WOT]

Your Guiding Words are your roots; they help you to stand tall and firm. Your action WOT are your daily drivers. They give you direction on how you can best live up to and work toward your Guiding Words.

It took me a long time to understand why I felt off-course or misguided or, frankly, sometimes just struggling to get through the day.

I was not giving myself any clear direction. I had no foundation.

Sure, I had a calendar that was full of to-do's, but honestly, there were days when I felt empty inside. To some this might sound cliché, but if you are reading this book, you know what I mean. You are giving your all at work, then coming home and doing your best to be with and raise your kids. And as much as you love your kids, they can also a source of stress, and some days one more thing to take care of.

I'm not saying this to be mean or make you feel bad. I'm saying this because I have been there. I would get up at 5 AM to exercise, shower and be out the door by 6:05 so I could make the express train into Boston. The moment I got on the train, I would open my laptop, and messages from the London office would be waiting. And most days, I would be on my phone and my laptop at the same time for the 50 minute train ride. I would grab a coffee, get into the office around 7:45 AM, and start my day: meetings, phone calls, team members, reports, clients . . . . Then I would run to catch the express train home and arrive at daycare to pick up my boys by 5:30 PM. That's over twelve hours already, and then dinner? Yup, had to make some of that, talk and play with the boys, get them into bed by 7:30 (if we were lucky) and then back to the laptop because there were always things left that I could "get to tonight." And at the end of the night, or especially on Friday nights, I would lay on the couch with my husband (both of us kind of watching the movie and kind of falling asleep at the same time) and wonder,

"WHAT AM I DOING?"

It finally dawned on me that I was running around like a chicken with its head cut off, with no clear direction. I was running in directions I thought I needed to be going, without asking myself if that's where I wanted to go. And it killed me! I had studied and worked too hard, put in the time, the effort, the hours, for it to all come to this!

Now, does any of that sound familiar?

That's when I took time to really assess who I was, what I wanted to do, what I liked to do. I brainstormed ways to bring all of those pieces of me together. And my idea of a foundation was born!

Because I like to keep things simple, I broke it down into overarching direction, or Guiding Words. Then, to keep me on track, I came up with my action WOT (Words of Today),that, unlike a to-do list, are actions or descriptors of who I want to be, and what I want to do that day.

Now, on to the work!

Within each phase there are steps, or building blocks. That is what you need to do to build the home you want to live in and share with others. The concept itself is simple, but going back to the basics is a little tough.

And that is why I wrote this book.

While this is the premise of my one of my coaching and workshop programs, everyone cannot be in one-on-one coaching with me or attend my workshops. So, after you have finished reading this book, completed the exercises and watched the videos, you will be on your path to Living Intentionally AND bringing balance to you and your family.

I realize some of you may still be skeptical or shaking your heads. And that's okay. It's natural, and I'm excited because that means I have your attention!

For the remainder of this book, I will take time to coach you through each of the phases and their respective building blocks. At the end of each chapter you will know:

- ❖ WHAT it is
- ❖ WHY you do it
- ❖ HOW to do it
- ❖ WHEN to do it
- ❖ WHAT you get out of it
- ❖ HOW you can share it and bring it to your family

Let's get started on building your foundation! We begin with your Guiding Words...

Chapter 4

How do you set your direction?

"They say actions speak louder than words, but sometimes it's those very words that determines what action you should take." –Rashid Rowe

The first question people ask me here is, *"What the heck are Guiding Words?"* I remember the first time I shared these with a client. Her response was, "What, am I lost?"

And my response was, "Well, yeah, sort of . . . ."

I know I've mentioned a few times already how your Guiding Words are not related to your to-do list or tasks to complete. And after reading this chapter, you will know why.

I wasn't kidding when I said your Guiding Words are your compass in life. Many of you are busy running from place to place and task to task without stopping to ask if all of what you are doing is serving *you*. I realize that you may not be able to do all of the things you'd like *all* of the time, but as Seth Godin asks in his blog, "Why do you do what you do?" Seth encourages the idea that even when we may not be doing something we absolutely enjoy—let's face it, there are just some things we *need* to do—it's not about *what* we are doing, but what we bring of ourselves that matters.

[Note: If you haven't read any of Seth's work, I highly recommend it; you should definitely subscribe to his blog! It is always short, sweet and to-the-point. Those of you who follow me on Facebook and LinkedIn are already familiar with Seth's work, as I share at least one of his posts a week. (And if you aren't a member, join me on Facebook and LinkedIn.)]

Do you bring passion and care into what you do?

That's where the magic of your Guiding Words comes in: the first part of building your foundation. In a moment, I will walk you through the first balancing act, and for this one, you should give yourself a few moments to sit, think and just take in what comes to mind.

Let me explain.

In essence, your Guiding Words are words that describe your truest, best self. They are words that you may not be living up to each day, but that you aspire to be. This description helps people put this exercise in perspective:

> *If you were to walk away from a meeting or from a conversation with friends, how would you want them to describe you? How would you like to be perceived? As strong or as 'wishy-washy?' As confident or as unsure of*

yourself? As caring or as someone who doesn't really think of others? As genuine or as someone who is out to get the most out of others without giving any of themselves?

I realize these are extreme examples, but I would venture a guess that no one wants to be perceived or described as not genuine, not caring, or out for themselves. Most would prefer positive aspects and traits. We are only human, and we have a need for groups and communities, but in order to be a part of the GOOD ones, we need to act and live accordingly.

So, are you ready? Let's get to the first balancing act and start building your foundation! I want to get the juices flowing. There are enough resources available out there for you to research the topic of Living Intentionally, but I *intend* (yup, pun intended) to make this as real and actionable as possible for you!

So, read the balancing act first, and then find a quiet space to complete it. I say this now because part of the challenge involves closing your eyes, and I don't want to be the cause of any accidents!

Your Guiding Words

Before you start this challenge, grab your journal or your downloadable workbook from your resources page: http://amysmalarz.com/book/

I would like for you to find a quiet space (if you aren't already in one), sit down, take a couple of deep breaths and relax. Now, I want you to think of three words that describe your truest, best self. When you walk away from a conversation, meeting, or party, you want to be described as those words.

They can be "strong," "smart," "confident," "caring," "bold," "passionate," "healthy," "giving," etc. What's important and CRITICAL here is that these are words you would like to be perceived as BEING. You may not feel you are living up to these words now, and that's okay. What's important is that you pick words that describe YOU and who YOU want to strive to be each and every day.

For this exercise, feel free to set the timer on your phone or computer. Give yourself three to five minutes to really think and play with words. You will be surprised by what words come to mind!

Okay, here we go . . . .

Find your quiet space, close your eyes, take some deep breaths and think about YOU.

Now that you have your three words, write them down!

Nice work! You have completed the first balancing act!

How does it feel to give yourself time to think about who you want to be?

What words did you write down?

How did you find this exercise?

Was it fun?

Did you come up with words that surprised you?

When was the last time you gave yourself some time to just sit and think about YOU, instead of what others say you need to be?

But you aren't done yet. The next step to laying your solid foundation is to bring your Guiding Words to life, to define them. You have found words that define you and even though you may have thought about why each word is important to you, I want to introduce the next balancing act.

Defining Your Guiding Words

Before you start this challenge, grab your journal or your downloadable workbook from your resources page: http://amysmalarz.com/book/

Now that you have written your three words down, it's time to write a sentence next to each one that says WHY each word is important to you. Write down your three words and write down why you picked those words. What do they mean to you? Why did you pick those words out of all the words swirling in your head?

I will share my own words and definitions as an example for you:

Present: I want to be 'in' every conversation and interaction I have. Whether it be with family, friends or colleagues—even strangers—I want to be in the moment and participate.

Passionate: I love what I do and I want people to feel that. I am truly excited to wake up each day and contribute! If people don't know that, then I'm not being my true self.

Bold: My dad always told me to 'stand up straight and look the world in the eye!' and it takes some meaning behind those words to make it happen. I am proud that I don't always take the road most traveled, that I try new things and stick behind what I say, even if it's not the most popular statement.

There are no right or wrong answers, but if these words have true meaning to you, writing down why they are important is easy!

Some science on why it works

I realize some of you, while feeling really good about this exercise, may stop and think,

> "Why do I need to do this?
> What's the point?"

I'm going to take a minute to share some science with you here.

It takes multiple exposures to an idea or thought for it to sink in. You may also know that writing things down increases your brain's ability to take it in, much more so than typing. That's why I asked you to not only write down your words once, but also a second time. The second time you are not only writing down your words, but what they mean to you. That action alone signals additional chemicals in your brain to pay attention. They scream, "This is important!"

And it *is* important, because for some of you, this may be the first time you have given yourself the time and space to really think about YOU. And for that alone I say congratulations, because that is a big accomplishment!

Once you have your Guiding Words and their meaning down, the next question you may ask is,

> "When do I use these words?"
> "How do I use these words?"

Yes, it feels great to have some self-definition and meaning associated with your Guiding Words, but you still need to connect the dots on how you can bring these words into each and every day.

When do use your Guiding Words?

Every day.

You probably saw that one coming, but it's true. While it is great to have Intentions, we need to turn them into action—and this is the first way to do that.

You need to have these three words at the top of your mind each and every day. There are a couple of tricks you can use to help you with that. One of them is to set an alarm on your phone. I suggest picking a time of day when you know you may get into a slump, or a common time when you take a break and find yourself wandering a bit. For me, those times are 10 AM and 3 PM. So I set my alarms for those times; here's how it works:

- ❖ Set an alarm on your phone for your desired time.
- ❖ On iPhone and Android, you can label your alarm. Put your three Guiding Words as your label. When the alarm goes off, you have to reach to your phone to turn it off. You'll see your Guiding Words.

The magic? You are forcing yourself to see your three Guiding Words at least twice a day—and what's even better is that you're reminding your body and brain of those words during the times of day when you are most likely to break away, get lost, or lose your course. It's a great time to ask:

> "Am I being my truest, best self right now?"
> "What else can I bring to contribute more and gain more enjoyment and fulfillment?"
> Am I living my Guiding Words right now?

Your "when" is up to you, but if you are new to this process, I suggest at least two times per day. If you have done this process before (or after you become familiar with it), you may set less alarms. Me? I like to keep consistent reminders, because as my nephew says, "Practice makes better practice!"

Another trick is to write out your words and make them visible to you each day. Whether they be on your bathroom or bedroom mirror, at your desk, on your wall, on your laptop, **it doesn't matter**. They just need to be in a place that's visible so you can be reminded of them each day. The more exposure you have to those words, the more they sink in, and the more they become a part of you. They become rooted and grounded—and that, my friend, is the beginning of a very, very solid foundation.

Which brings us to the next balancing act . . . .

Seeing Your Guiding Words

Before you start this challenge, grab your journal or your downloadable workbook from your resources page: http://amysmalarz.com/book/

Put your words where others can see them: on your mirror, in your office, in your bedroom—wherever. Talk about them with your kids to your spouse. While some may find it hokey at first, the idea can be catchy!

Get an index card and write them out, print them out, color them in—however you want to do it. Just write them out and put them where you can see them each and every day.

Where are you going to put your Guiding Words to keep you on course?

How do use your Guiding Words?

I alluded to this in the previous section, but honestly, these words are there to help you right your ship. Remember that you are off-course 99 percent of the time, and it's up to you to get back on course.

Seeing your Guiding Words each and every day is exactly how you'll stay—or get back—on course.

In a recent conversation with a client, I asked her about her Guiding Words, and she said,

> "I have been using my Guiding Words to keep me focused. I have been using them for framing situations, handling situations and for thinking about how I want to be perceived after leaving. Let's just say they have come in handy a bunch of times, even just this week!"

Remember, it's about consistently and continually acting how you want to be perceived. There's no magic bullet. And if you want to build a solid foundation that will be able to weather any storm, it all starts here.

The benefits of Guiding Words

I could go on for days about the benefits of guiding words. Instead, I would like to share a couple of stories with you about people who are not only using their Guiding Words, but whose Guiding Words have helped them along their journey.

One of my clients is an accomplished CPA, but he wanted to explore writing a book to help other dads be better dads. He'd learned a lot of lessons throughout his lifetime, and now, being a parent for the second time, he wanted to share them with others. Perhaps like many of you, when he first went through his Guiding Words exercise, he felt silly and wasn't really sure what it would do for him. But he did it anyway. After a couple of weeks he came back to me and said,

> "The one thing that had the greatest impact on me so far in this challenge is seeing the massive impact of "grow" words flowing through me each day. The whole process has been very eye-opening [for me] because it has redefined my daily actions and added more accountability on myself, which I love."

And I have many other stories similar to his. Just by giving yourself time to get back to YOU, exploring how you really want to not only be perceived, but show up in the world, can make dramatic shifts. Reece said himself that he is redefining his actions (we will learn more about how to do that in the next chapter) and holding himself to greater accountability!

Now, I never said to him that he would need to redefine his actions—he came to that on his own. I never said he would need to think of accountability measures—he did *that* on his own. And that is the amazing part: when we find something we love, care and are passionate about, following that path is easy.

It's only hard when we don't want to go that way but feel we *have* to. When you start building your foundation and have your Guiding Words, you are on your way toward actions and activities that serve you better.

Why not make it easier on yourself?

Oh, and it's not just you that will benefit . . . .

How to influence your family

If you are a parent, you may have skipped to this part first. And if you did, go back and do the balancing acts in this chapter, then come back.

But if you followed along, let's talk about how doing this for yourself can bring balance to your family.

Like the airlines say, put on your own oxygen mask first before helping others. This is the same when it comes to family. You have to build your own Home and work on your own balance before you can ask others to do the same.

People best learn by example, and this is no different. You must *lead* by example so your family can learn.

When you Live Intentionally, you bring balance to yourself and eventually to those around you. It's amazing how it works, but people around you will feel your Intent and may want to go along for the ride. Or some may take a step back. It can be intimidating for others when they know you have Intention—and there are no apologies for that.

And when it comes to family—especially children—we want to set a good example. I know I feel that way with my two sons. I want them to respect and love themselves and others. I want them to explore and experience life! One way I help them is by sharing my Guiding Words and leading by example.

The best and simplest way to influence your family is to be the model of what you want for them.

If you want your loved ones to have a solid foundation, you need one, too.

If you want your loved ones to think about, write down and remind themselves of their Guiding Words, you need to do that, too.

If you want your family to take themselves seriously, to love and respect themselves, then you need to love and respect yourself, too.

I know I've said this before, and I'll say it again: it's simple but not always easy. But like riding a bike, the more you do it, the better you become, the easier it is, the less energy it takes to get up and go . . . and keep going.

When your kids were learning to tie their shoelaces (my youngest just figured that one out not too long ago), you didn't tell them to stop trying. You encouraged them to keep at it, to keep practicing! This is no different, yet so often we treat it differently. We treat ourselves as afterthoughts. It's time to stop that behavior, and it's time to start thinking about, writing down and living our Guiding Words each and every day!

You might think it's easier for me because my kids are younger, but you would be surprised. One of my clients, Jillian, shared this story with me and gave me permission to share it with you.

> "I went through Amy's process of thinking of and defining my Guiding Words. That part was easy. As much as I love my kids and husband, the hardest part was actually sharing these words with those that I loved. And I think the reason they were so hard to share with them is because . . . well, because what they think of me matters so much. What if the words I chose for myself were so far off-course that they laughed, or maybe even worse, just said, 'Oh, that's nice . . . .' I knew they saw me as a mom and wife, but what if they didn't see me as I wanted the most important people in my world, my life, to see me? It was a big leap of faith to share my three Guiding Words, but wow, it was one of the best things I ever did! They not only saw those traits, those words in me, but they would remind me of those words, sometimes even when I didn't want to be reminded! And maybe even best of all, each of my three kids and my husband decided to join me and pick three Guiding Words of their own."

And I can say from my own experiences, my kids have a lot of fun coming up with words to describe our family. We share lots of smiles and it's also been a great way to get to know my kids even better!

This brings me to the next balancing act . . . .

Your Family's Guiding Words

Before you start this challenge, grab your journal or your downloadable workbook from your resources page: http://amysmalarz.com/book/

The idea here is to come up with some family Guiding Words. This is a nice step to sharing with your family, because they don't need to come up with words individually. Instead, you come up with words together!

How does your family want to be perceived in your neighborhood? Your community? How do you want to contribute?

Get some index cards and some markers or crayons and write your words out, print them out, color them in—however you want to do it. Just write them out and then put them where you can see them each and every day.

Where are you going to put your family Guiding Words to keep you on course?

Great job!

What words did they come up with?

Do you feel like a stronger family unit after doing this?

Now that you have the first part of your foundation finished, let's move on to the second part, your action Words of Today [WOT]!

Chapter 5

How do you turn your Intentions into action?

"Words may show a man's wit, but actions his meaning." –Benjamin Franklin

It is critical to have words to follow, to help you along. And in this case, it's necessary because it helps your foundation to take shape. Yet words can only take you so far. It's turning them into action that can be a bigger challenge.

I hear this a LOT. In fact, that is one of the main reasons I started my podcast, "Living Intentionally with Amy Smalarz." I want to know how each of my guests define Living Intentionally and how they turn their words or thoughts into actions each and every day.

This is such an interesting topic to explore, which is why my next book is dedicated to it, but here, in this book, in this point of the process, I want to equip you with the tools to turn your Guiding Words into what I love to call your action WOT [Words of Today].

What are action WOT?

All of this came about because it was great to have my Guiding Words to help me keep my momentum going when I needed it . . . but that wasn't enough.

That's when I came up with the idea of my WOT. Some of you may be familiar with WOD, or CrossFit lingo for "Work Out of the Day". I have some great friends who own CrossFit gyms and others who go religiously. One day, on the soccer field, I was talking with a parent during our kids' games, and the conversation went to her WOD. She was talking about how she really enjoys going because she gets something new or fresh every day—but all with the same goal of making her stronger.

And it hit me! Why not have action WOT every day to keep me on track, to make my mind stronger? If it works for them and their bodies, heck, it would work for me and my mind!

I not only brought this idea to myself, but shared it with some of my clients, like Karen. Karen had participated in one of my online challenges and then moved on to one of my coaching programs. When I asked her about the action WOT, she said,

> "The biggest takeaway for me overall has been the opportunity over a series of days to really think about what it means to be more Intentional in my life. Juggling a lot of balls, I really need to be more focused each day on my WOT! This has been powerful, and it is all keenly important in the cycle and mindset of living with Intention!"

And you may be thinking, hey, all of this is great—in theory! But how or where do I even begin to think about and define my action WOT?

Good news—I'm about to tell you.

How do come up with your action WOT?

This is a place a lot of people get stuck. Thinking of Guiding Words—sure. You can think longer-term and visualize those. But it can be harder (and even a bit draining) to say, "I'm going to have to do this each and every day?" And you may also be asking,

How the heck do I do that?
What if I run out of words?!

The idea of your action WOT is to have at least one word for each day that describes an action you need or want to take, but in a positive light. Here's an example. Today, I am working on my book, so my action WOT is WRITING. It's an action that describes what I want to be doing, and it feels positive to me. You will notice that I did not say "write a chapter." That is something you would find on a to-do list, and that is not what action WOT are for.

The purpose of the action WOT is to give you at least one active word that you feel good about, that reminds you of what you want to accomplish or work toward completing that day. It's not a word that can be checked off at the end of the day;

rather, it's a word that you can look back on to ask yourself, "Did I take that action today?"

Some days my words are "teaching" or "learning" or "workshop leading.". Other days, the only word on my sheet of paper is "surviving" because that is how I'm feeling. But you know what? That's okay, because it's an active word that's positive. You can pick words that reflect where you are, but also that keep your mindset in a positive direction.

Again, this is a place where I occasionally lose people, so let's go straight to the next balancing act.

Your action WOT [Words of Today]

Before you start this challenge, grab your journal or your downloadable workbook from your resources page: http://amysmalarz.com/book/

Think of things you would like to do tomorrow (or today, if it's early morning). They can be things you want to do, need to do, or both. A good place to start is with a to-do list (if you use one). Take a look at what you see in front of you, and think about a word (or words) that **positively** describe what you would like to accomplish.

Write them down.

Now you have your action WOT!

Remember, the purpose of the action WOT is to give you an active word that you feel good about. It should remind you of what you want to accomplish or work toward completing that day. Your Guiding Words describe how you want to show up each day and contribute to the world; your action WOT are the daily steps you take to keep yourself on course, in your own direction.

When do you come up with your action WOT?

The next question many people ask is,

"What is the best or ideal time to come up with my action WOT?"

I will share with you what I tell my clients. I turn it back to them and ask,

"What would work best for you?"

Yeah, I know—not much help, right? I can narrow it down for you and say that I have found two different times of day to be the most ideal:

- ❖ Early in the morning.
- ❖ In the evening, before going to bed.

For those of you who like to plan your day in the morning, or at least think about what's up for the day, then early in the morning will most likely work the best for you. And it's easier to think about and write down your action WOT alongside your to-do list. You are already writing down things you want to accomplish, so this is an ideal time to turn some of those items on your to-do list into positive action words!

If you are someone who likes to take time at night to think and plan ahead, then the evening is a better time for you. Again, you are already in the mind-frame of putting together a to-do list, so it's an ideal time to turn some of those items on your list into positive action words!

[NOTE: I am not a proponent of to-do lists, per se, and there are many methods and apps to help you compose those. I don't talk about that in this book, but I bring it up because I know many of you use them and are familiar with them. I know that grounding or routing new practices with things you are already used to doing can help with the transition.]

On to the next balancing act . . . .

Balancing Act

Your Time for Action WOT

Before you start this challenge, grab your journal or your downloadable workbook from your resources page: http://amysmalarz.com/book/

Now it's time to think about and write down when you will develop your action WOT.

I suggest picking early morning or in the evening before bed.

When thinking about your preferred time of day, pick one that you are willing to stick with for seven days. If after the seven days it feels to hard or you are not keeping up with the practice, switch to the other time of day and see how that feels.

The key is NOT to switch every day, but to "pick it and stick it."

What time of day will you write down your action WOT?

Write that down, and let's continue!

Great! I'm glad you have written down a time of day when you will think about and write down your action WOT. Honestly, that is the hardest part. When you give yourself time and direction, it's amazing what happens! All you have to do is follow your own lead!

This brings me to you and your family.

How can you share your action WOT?

Just like I mentioned in the previous chapter, the best way to share your action WOT with your family is talk about yours, and maybe even more importantly, act them out each day. Your loved ones will see your actions and feel them. They will start to notice some changes—positive ones—and they may even ask you what you are doing differently. This is a great opportunity to share your process with them.

But what if they don't ask?

One way to share the idea of action WOT is to talk about them during family meals. I don't know about you, but in my house, there are some days we struggle to have time to all sit together. And then when we are sitting together, it can be more of a "necessary exercise" instead of having family time. So I came up with a way to make it fun and light—to make conversation and to get responses back, at least for a majority of the time. Instead of asking how their day went, I ask questions like,

"Who made you smile today?"
"Who did you help today?"

More often than not, that will naturally lead to a story, because it's hard to just give a name and not share the context. Once they get talking and I'm listening (critical step) the rest falls into place. And yes, this works for people of all ages (kids and spouses included). This is also a great place to pick out an action WOT for them and say something like,

> "Wow, you were such a great **helper** in class today!"
> "What a great example of how to be a **listener** to a friend when they needed you."

See how this can work? By using words like "helper" and "listener," you are giving them their own action WOT and reinforcing it in a positive way.

Another practical tool that I use is a whiteboard.

In our kitchen, we have a whiteboard where we take turns writing down an inspirational quote or drawing a picture.. It's right there in the kitchen, so it's guaranteed that everyone will see it at some point during the day. I started to write down one of my action WOT on the board. Some days my kids ask about it, others they don't. But every time they do ask, it's a teachable moment. And, bonus, I ask the kids at the end of the day if they think I acted on my WOT. They love that because it flips the roles a bit: they get to assess how Mama did, instead of being asked how they're doing all of the time. And they become cheerleaders, too, because they want me to be successful. It's a win-win!

Now, before you get any "Norman Rockwell" pictures in your head, these scenarios don't play out every day. But four to five days a week, it works. When we first started, it was one, maybe two days a week. But like anything else, after practicing for a while, it starts to stick. It becomes routine. It becomes a part of you and a part of your family. It becomes something you do together—a grounding point, something you share.

And, hey, isn't that what family is all about? And with that in mind, we move on to the final balancing act for this chapter.

Sharing Your Family Action WOT

Before you start this challenge, grab your journal or your downloadable workbook from your resources page: http://amysmalarz.com/book/

I provided the dinner table question and whiteboard examples of how I share and talk about action WOT. This is how I work each day to include my family. These may work for you; they may not.

Take a few minutes to brainstorm what you can do at home to share your action WOT with your family.

What can you do to include them, pique their interest, and maybe even get them started on their own action WOT?

Remember, there are no right or wrong answers here.

What might work for you?

Whatever you come up with, try it for a week. Combine it with the previous chapter challenge.

Write down your action WOT at the same time every day, and then try your idea for sharing it with your family.

And there you have it! You have your foundation! You have your three Guiding Words that describe your truest, best self. And now you have your daily action WOT!

Before moving onto Phase II, take a few minutes to review your foundation.

→ How does it feel?

◆ Does it feel good?

◆ Do you feel strong?

◆ Do you feel like you can weather any storm?

You've started building your own Home. You should take a moment to congratulate yourself! Completing this first phase is critical because you are working on your own foundation, then modeling it for others. It is quite an accomplishment.

Having said that, we cannot stop here! We must continue . . . .

Are you ready?

Let's head to Phase II: Your Support!

Phase II:

Your Support

"A house is made with walls and beams; a home is built with love and dreams."

–Ralph Waldo Emerson

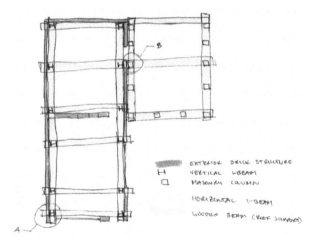

EXTERIOR BRICK STRUCTURE

VERTICAL I-BEAM

MASONRY COLUMN

HORIZONTAL I-BEAM

WOODEN BEAM (ROOF SUPPORT)

Chapter 6

What is your support?

This phase is where a lot of rubber meets the road. This is where your work comes into play. Once you have your foundation, you can use it to set up your support systems—and that's why it needs to be strong and truly a part of you.

In the next couple of chapters, you will learn how to prioritize your "important" versus their "urgent" and how to use your Decision Tree when it comes to thinking about potential opportunities.

I will share simple exercises with you, but like many simple things, the devil is in the details. I turn traditional management training on its head, and then I give you the tools to make better decisions.

We are faced with thousands of decisions each day, and making all of them can get exhausting. But after you finish reading the next two chapters, you will see how you can not only get more fulfillment and enjoyment out of your days, but also how you can get some of your time back!

Remember, time is precious. Unlike money, once you spend it, you can never get it back, so you need to spend it wisely.

Are you ready for the first support system: your "important" versus their "urgent?"

Chapter 7

How do you get more of your "important" and less of their "urgent?"

"It's never too late to realize what's important in your life and to fight for it."
– Unknown

"What is important is seldom urgent, and what is urgent is seldom important."
– Dwight Eisenhower, 34th President of the United States

You have lots to do each day—or at least you think you do.

I'm not trying to be critical here, but by the end of this chapter, I venture to guess that you will see you have more time than you now think.

You are just giving too much of it away.

The Eisenhower Box

In a 1954 speech to the Second Assembly of the World Council of Churches, former US President Dwight D. Eisenhower, who was quoting Dr. J. Roscoe Miller (President of Northwestern University) said, "I have two kinds of problems: the urgent and the important. The urgent are not important, and the important are never urgent." This "Eisenhower Principle" is said to be how he organized his

workload and priorities.[1]

THE EISENHOWER BOX

	URGENT	NOT URGENT
IMPORTANT	**DO** *Do it now.* Write article for today.	**DECIDE** *Schedule a time to do it.* Exercising. Calling family and friends. Researching articles. Long-term biz strategy.
NOT IMPORTANT	**DELEGATE** *Who can do it for you?* Scheduling interviews. Booking flights. Approving comments. Answering certain emails. Sharing articles.	**DELETE** *Eliminate it.* Watching television. Checking social media. Sorting through junk mail.

Many of you may have learned this in school, or perhaps been exposed to it in one

of your management trainings or meetings. This picture may look familiar.

While I agree with the "Delegate: and "Delete" quadrants (we all need more of those

in our lives), I want to focus on the "Do" and "Decide" quadrants.

Let me ask you a couple of questions:

1) How many of you DO what is important to you? At least one "important" thing a day?

2) Now, how many of you "Decide" to DO what's important to you . . . *tomorrow?*

---

[1] https://www.mindtools.com/pages/article/newHTE_91.htm

Can I get a smile or at least a smirk?

I hope you can appreciate the questions and why I asked them. Unfortunately, many of you use the Eisenhower Box to "*Decide*" to put off what is important to you.

Tricky, isn't it? You are tricking yourself into thinking that you are actually doing something, when in reality, all you are doing is putting off what is "important" to you!

Your "important" versus their "urgent"

Before getting into the nitty-gritty details of the chapter, I want to share definitions I like to use for "urgent" and "important."

Urgent = Requires immediate action or attention

Important = Something of great significance or value; likely to have a profound effect on success, survival, or well-being

After reading these definitions, which would you prefer to have more of in your life? Personally, "important" is what gets me up in the morning and what keeps me going throughout the day. And I'm guessing it might be the same for you . . . *if* you had more "important" in your life.

Which brings me to the next balancing act . . . .

Balancing Act

Your "Urgent" versus "Important" Definitions

Before you start this challenge, grab your journal or your downloadable workbook from your resources page: http://amysmalarz.com/book/

Now, it's your turn to write down your definition of "urgent" and "important."

You can copy the ones I shared with you, but I encourage you to make them your own—even just by changing a word or two.

Putting them into your own words gives them real, true meaning to you.

So go ahead, write them down!

Earlier in the book, I shared the story of my day—or at least an overview of it. Train ride to Boston. Meetings all day. Clients and team members to work with. Train ride home. Pick up kids from after school care. Have some sort of dinner. Get ready for bed. Bedtime. Rinse . . . lather . . . repeat.

Those were my days.

Now, don't get me wrong; there were team members and clients I really enjoyed working with. We even shared laughs, cries and friendships.

94

And my kids—wow! Picking them up from daycare was the highlight of my day. Seeing their smiling faces and feeling their little arms around me just gave me a huge jolt of love and energy. And at bedtime, the stories the kids would share as they were falling asleep would teach me more about them and their minds in the last fifteen minutes of the day than I may have known hours before. And then what felt like fleeting moments with my husband at night . . . .Those were my days.

But, in between all of that, let's be honest—the rest of my day was filled with urgency. I was so, so busy. I had meetings to attend, remember? I had things to get done, things to check off my list. And if I didn't do all of this, often times, stuff just wouldn't get done—or so I thought.

And the emails—oh, the emails. Not to mention what Dave and I used to call "dueling laptops" at night. You know: when you're pretending to share time with your spouse or partner, but in reality you're working (or at least checked out from them). Sure, I was sitting next to him, but we were only sharing space, not time, together.

And then Friday afternoon would come around, and I would be tired. I'd first think, "Wow, I did a lot this week!" But when I'd relax, give myself a few moments of quiet, and really think back on what I had done, I soon became a bit disappointed in what I discovered.

I could say that I got a lot of *other* people's things done, but when it came down to things I felt were important—like getting in that longer run each week or reading that book on my shelf or finishing up a certification or getting home early to have real time with the family—all of those seemed to fall by the wayside.

I always DECIDED I would do those things, but more often than not, I ended up "Doing" what was "urgent" for others.

Take back your "important!"

That's when I really decided that I would include at least one thing a day that was "important" to me. Mind you, I wasn't exactly sure how I would do this on a consistent basis, but once I get something in my head, I'm pretty much going to do it!

Then it hit me! I was making a to-do list each morning, so I just added one more column to that list and wrote down U/I. U for "urgent" and I for "important." After writing down my tasks or items to complete for the day, I would then circle the U or the I.

Pretty simple, huh? And multi-purpose. Remember earlier when I was sharing a tip on coming up with your action WOT? Well, you can use your to-do list not only to help with your action WOT, but also to identify and hone in on YOUR "important!"

But full disclosure—I have to admit something. And this may happen to you, too.

That first day, I was devastated. I'd circled U for every single item on my daily planner. There were no I's for "important" to be found. Anywhere.

I felt defeated . . . for a moment. But then it came to me—why not ADD something to my list that was important to me? That way I would have at least one I on my list circled, and if nothing else, I would feel better!

And so it began: my daily ritual of including at least one I task or item each day. And let me tell you how liberating that was. I gave myself permission to do at least one thing a day for me, and I have never looked back.

You want to know what the first item was? Five minutes to just sit. Sit by myself and not have to do anything, get anything, say anything, think anything . . . just sit.

You see, it doesn't have to be anything super big or monumental. Just something for YOU. While writing this book, I asked my clients what's on their "important" list (it's one of the first questions I ask) and here's what they shared:

- → A bath
- → A walk around the block
- → Haircut, manicure, pedicure
- → Playing soccer with the kids
- → Glass of wine on the deck
- → Writing a blog post
- → A nap
- → Reading a chapter a day of my book
- → Playing a video game
- → Facebook
- → Remodeling their bathroom (this one gives me flashbacks.)

I could go on, but I think you get the picture. It doesn't matter necessarily what it is, but what's important is that it is something YOU want to do.

Now it's your turn to imagine and even act!

On to the next balancing act . . . .

Your ME Activities

Before you start this challenge, grab your journal or your downloadable workbook from your resources page: http://amysmalarz.com/book/

Take a moment to think about a day when you recently did something for yourself. What did you do?

What is something you can do today or maybe for each day this week—for you?

Write them down. Write down as many that come to your mind.

And because this one tends to be more difficult, give yourself three minutes to write. Don't pick up that pen until the three minutes are up!

Be Selfish

Before moving on, I would like to take moment to talk about selfishness.

I bring this up because I have been called selfish for doing something each day for me. And you may have had a small voice in your head calling you the same thing. Or at least a tiny voice that says,

> "You can't do that! Do you know what needs to get done?
>
> How can you take time to do THAT when everyone else is waiting for something or needing something?"

I know, because I used to hear those voices pretty much every day. But now, after giving myself a taste of doing things for me, I can't go back. And because I've given myself ME time, I bring more joy into the other areas of my life. Because I'm taking time for me, I have a better sense of who I am and what drives me.

Which brings me to the next section: working and dealing with other people's "urgent." You know it's there, and for many of you, you can't avoid it completely. But I'm here to say that while it may be a part of your life, it doesn't have to be the main or only part.

Their "urgent"

No lie, I just had this conversation with a client the other day. Her exact words were,

> *"Aligning my "urgent"/"important" with others' "urgent"/"important" is hard. Sometimes when I put my "important" ahead of someone else's "urgent," I get in trouble . . . ."*

I'm guessing she's not alone. Actually, I can say that she isn't alone—none of us are.

It can be scary to take time for yourself. If it isn't scary, it's at least out of your element. But it's important to do it. It keeps things in perspective and helps you to start creating a balance.

There is also something really important I want to point out from Amanda's statement. She acknowledged that she has "important" versus "urgent" tasks to take care of that may not be in alignment with someone else's "important" versus "urgent." And that other person can be your spouse, your kids, your boss, your co-worker, your neighbor, or your friend.

While others may not be working on their "important," they certainly have their list of "urgent!" And not surprisingly, that may not be, or probably isn't, in alignment with your "important."

Therein lies the balance of keeping your "important" at front of mind and making that part of your day *while* balancing others' "urgent" or what they call "important" (which is probably just an "urgent" that was due yesterday).

This brings me to the next balancing act!

The People in Your Life

Before you start this challenge, grab your journal or your downloadable workbook from your resources page: http://amysmalarz.com/book/

Now is time to write down the people in your life who you interact with on a daily and weekly basis.

The purpose of this exercise is to become aware of all of the people in your life who may be competing with your attention.

It's not on purpose or malicious, but they will want things from you. And the more you give to others, the less you have for yourself.

It's time to take inventory so you know what you are up against.

Take some time to think about people you live with, work with, and interact with, and write them down.

Write down their name, your relationship with them, and what they usually ask of you.

Remember to take your time and come up with as many people and scenarios as you can think of.

Leading by example

→ Let's do a quick recap:

→ You have defined what "important" and "urgent" mean to you.

→ You have come up with some things that are "important" to you that you can do for yourself.

→ You have thought about and written down a list of people who rely on you and what you do for them.

Such great work! You should be proud of yourself for doing all of the work you have done so far. And now comes the next step of taking all of this work and knowledge beyond yourself and bringing it to your family.

As the title of this section suggests, it's a way of leading by example. One trick I use with my kids (which drives them bonkers, so I highly recommend it!) is as follows:

Child: "Mama, I need *(a glass of milk, new sneakers, or who knows what)*."

Me: "Okay, I hear what you're saying. Is this something you absolutely need or something you would like to have?"

NOTE: This question alone results in a potential rolling of the eyes because they know what's coming.

Child: "Mama, I just need it . . . ."

Me: "Okay, so it sounds like something you would like to have, not something you would die without."

Child: "[Sigh] Mama, no, I don't need to have it, but I would like to have it. May I please have [insert whatever they were asking for in the first place]?"

At this point, I consider helping them with it or suggest they have two legs and can get up and get it themselves . . . nicely, of course.

I am having some fun here, but I hope you get the gist of the conversation. I don't say "yes" immediately, but instead push back on them to get at *why* they are asking for whatever they're asking for. You can do the same for anyone: kids, boss, spouse, friend, neighbor, and so on. Asking these questions is a signal that I have things to do, too, and I am not at the beck and call of everyone all of the time.

Don't overlook that . . . it's important for others to know that.

And as an added bonus, my boys are learning to do things for themselves and becoming beautiful, strong, independent-thinking little people.

On to the next balancing act . . . .

Your Important Conversations

Before you start this challenge, grab your journal or your downloadable workbook from your resources page: http://amysmalarz.com/book/

I gave the example of a conversation I have with my children pretty much on a daily basis.

Now it's your turn!

What could you say to your kids, your boss or your co-worker when asked to do something?

It may feel strange at first, but trust me, visualizing something ahead of time works wonders when the time comes for the real thing.

Okay, get out that journal and give it a go!

It is possible!

I wanted to end this chapter on a high note. One of my clients recently shared his

insight when it comes to his "important" versus their "urgent."

> "I was definitely a user of the old style of "urgent" versus "important." Daily I
> have a list in my work life that I just write, delegate, plan or do. But I love the
> new concept of "important" versus "urgent." It makes it easier to draw the line
> of what is what. I will definitely be using this and giving it a go tomorrow when
> I'm back at work!"

It is possible!

It's really amazing what can happen when you have your foundation, or your

Guiding Words and action WOT. You are able to begin building your support

systems and putting them into place.

Deciphering and being clear on what is "important" and what is "urgent" is the first

part of your support. We are going to move on to the second part, your Decision

Tree.

As you will see, it's near impossible to make "good" decisions without these other

pieces in place. So, without further ado, let's learn why and how you can make

better decisions—more easily and with much less stress!

Chapter 8

How do you make better, faster and easier decisions?

"A bird sitting on a tree is never afraid of the branch breaking, because her trust is not on the branch but on her own wings. Always believe in yourself." – Unknown

Unsuccessful people make decisions based on their current situation. Successful people make decisions based on where they want to be." – *Unknown*

Do you know how you make decisions? I don't mean your process of selecting the red shirt versus the black one. I mean, do you know how your brain and body work to make decisions?

You may or may not be aware of this, but you make decisions emotionally first, and then the logical part of your brain kicks in to rationalize your emotional decision.

Don't believe me? Read Daniel Kahneman's *Thinking, Fast and Slow* because he does an amazing job presenting decades of research. He and his colleagues spent decades reading about and conducting their own research on this topic, and honestly, it's fascinating. Here is an excerpt from the introduction:

> "When you are asked what you are thinking about, you can normally answer. You believe you know what goes on in your mind, which often consists of one conscious thought leading in an orderly way to another. But that is not the only way the mind works, nor indeed the typical way. Most impressions and thoughts arise in your conscious experience without your knowing how they got there. You cannot race how you came to the belief that there is a lamp on the desk in front of you, or how you detected a hint of irritation in your

spouse's voice on the telephone, or how you managed to avoid a threat on the road before you became consciously aware of it. The mental work that produces impressions, intuitions and many decisions goes on in silence in our mind.

Much of the discussion in [Thinking, Fast and Slow] this book is about biases of intuition   As we navigate our lives, we normally allow ourselves to be guided by impressions and feelings and the confidence we have in our intuitive beliefs and preferences is usually justified. But not always. We are often confident even when we are wrong   " (page 4, Thinking, Fast and Slow)

We are faced with thousands of decisions each day, and frankly, making so many decisions can get exhausting! I don't know about you, but some days, by midday, I'm done having to make decisions. The trouble is, each day we are faced with many, many small decisions—and then there are the bigger ones we need to give more time and attention to. But if we rush it, or don't have a process to give ourselves time to think, to catch up with what we feel, then we may make what could be seen as a 'wrong' decision down the road.

Think about a recent opportunity that came your way. It could be volunteering for your kid's school, joining a board, taking a new job, going to yoga class, or going out for a girls'/guys' night. Each of these represent an opportunity. And when we are presented with something, we can't help but become emotionally attached, either positively or negatively, to that opportunity.

Now I want you to keep that in mind and use it for the next balancing act.

Your Opportunity

Before you start this challenge, grab your journal or your downloadable workbook from your resources page: http://amysmalarz.com/book/

Take a moment to list one, two, or three recent opportunities. They should be something you had to think about before committing.

Write them down.

Now take a moment to think about the opportunity and write down how it made you feel. Were you excited? Were you anxious? Was it something you dreaded?

Write down your emotion and say whether that emotion was positive or negative.

Now that you have gone through this process for yourself, let me share a personal story with you.

Not too long ago (just about three years ago, in fact), I was presented with an opportunity to serve on the board of a local co-op school. This school is amazing, and I'm proud to say my kids had the good fortune to go and be a part of its community. Now, at the same time, I had recently launched my business, become an associate professor, and volunteered to be the room parent for both of my sons' classrooms.

Ridiculous, right? My husband thought so, too—and told me as much—but I was so emotionally attached and excited, how could I say no?

[NOTE: Easy: just say "no." Or at least, "I'll think about it."]

I'd always wanted to be an active member of the community and to "give back" or contribute. Not to mention the fact that I truly believe in the school's mission and philosophy. Children learn by playing, trying things out, experimenting with different materials and ways of doing things. They have to figure things out together, from how to make pancakes to the rules of the classroom.

But I didn't have the right tool, my Decision Tree, in my hands yet. I got so caught up in the emotional aspect of being a member of the Board that I didn't take time to think. I rationalized my decision to overload my schedule to be on the Board by thinking everything else would work itself out.

So while I don't necessarily regret the decision I made, I may have made a better one if I'd had this tool.

Your Decision Tree

I absolutely LOVE this tool, and you will, too! It's a one-page cheat sheet on making decisions. (See http://amysmalarz.com/book/ to download your copy.)

It's so simple, yet so powerful.

DECISION TREE

MY OPPORTUNITY IS:

MY 3 GUIDE WORDS ARE:

THIS OPPORTUNITY WILL BRING ME:

BY TAKING THIS OPPORTUNITY, I WILL SACRIFICE/GIVEUP:

THIS IS A (CIRCLE ONE) OPPORTUNITY:

GROWTH   OR   DEPLETING

It's a five-step process to help you make a decision—hence, your Decision Tree. Before you go through an exercise on your own—as that is the next balancing act—let's walk through it together.

STEP 1: Write down your opportunity

The first step is to write down the opportunity you have been given. It can be big or small. It can be joining a board, it can be going to an exercise class, it can be having a date night (one of my personal favorites) or it can be accepting that job offer. The critical piece of this is to write down the opportunity in YOUR OWN words.

STEP #2: Your Guiding Words

The second step is to write down your three Guiding Words. (See, I told you they would come in handy!) Remember, these words are your foundation. They are words that remind you of your truest, best self—who you want to be and how you are working to be perceived each day. You write each of them down here.

STEP #3: Benefits of the Opportunity

The third step is to write down, in YOUR OWN words, what this opportunity will bring you. Put it all out there: the good, the bad or the ugly. Use your gut for this one.

→ What feelings come to the surface when you think about this opportunity?
→ Why are you even considering it in the first place?

This is important to write down because your mind is already thinking these thoughts, and writing them down gives you time to process them.

STEP #4: What you will have to sacrifice or give up

Now here comes the tough love. The fourth step is to write down what you will have to sacrifice or give up in order to take advantage of this opportunity.

[NOTE: You need to be brutally honest. Don't hold back here, because you are only hurting yourself in the long run if you do. Think of worse-case scenarios. What will you really have to give up or have less of? You cannot skip this step, because if you do, you are only cheating yourself in the process. It is placed right after the benefits because it is a way for you to create balance in your brain and then your emotions.]

When you are writing this section, you may feel calm or like you are losing your steam. You may even start to feel deflated. That's okay! It's better to go through that now than after starting. That's why it is here.

I was talking to a client the other day, and he shared his "sacrifice" with me. I'd like to share it with you now.

> "My opportunity is to write a chapter in a book with other colleagues. The opportunity will bring additional exposure as a writer and help encourage others on their journey. By taking this opportunity, though, I will have to sacrifice two weeks of sleep and family time. But I made the decision to go forward with and accept this opportunity because it was something I didn't want to give up."

While he was excited about the opportunity, he recognized that he would give up some sleep and his family time, neither of which are things you can get back.

Which leads me to the last step: the decision.

STEP #5: Growth or Depleting Opportunity

Up to this point, you have:

- → Written down what the opportunity is, in your own words
- → Used your three Guiding Words
- → Written down the benefits (what this opportunity will bring to you) in your own words
- → Written down the sacrifice (what you will need to give up or not do in order to take this opportunity)

Now it's game time! In the end, after you have gone through all of this, it's time to decide whether this opportunity is a GROWTH opportunity or a DEPLETING one.

- → A **GROWTH** opportunity is one that is in alignment with your Guiding Words and one that is worth the sacrifice. You will get more out of it than you have to give up.
- → A **DEPLETING** opportunity is one that does not take you in the direction of your Guiding Words and one that is not worth the sacrifice.

That's it. It's really that simple. And in simplicity there is beauty.

Remember, I mentioned that we make decisions based on our emotions first and then use logic to rationalize our decisions. Using this tool allows you to write down your emotional stuff and then bring your logical side up to speed—all on one page.

Remember my story about the local co-op board? If I'd had this tool back then, I probably would have politely declined the position. While I was flattered and excited, if I had taken the time to really think it through, it probably would have surfaced that I just didn't have the bandwidth to sacrifice. Not to mention the idea that it would have brought to mind other things I was probably overextending myself on.

This tool can be a life-saver.

Now it's your turn,. Take a stab at filling out your own Decision Tree. Remember, some people find it easier to start with the "smaller" stuff, like getting a babysitter for that date night or for that exercise class. Others like to go straight to the big ones, like accepting a job offer or starting that new business venture. Whichever way you'd like to approach it, the only "right" way is to start!

Your Opportunity

Before you start this challenge, grab your journal or your downloadable workbook from your resources page: http://amysmalarz.com/book/

Now it's your turn to try this out, to go through the process of your own Decision Tree.

Follow the steps:

Step 1: Write down the opportunity in your own words.

Step 2: Write down your three Guiding Words.

Step 3: Write down what benefits you will receive from the opportunity.

Step 4: Write down what you will need to give up or sacrifice for the opportunity.

Step 5: Write down (or circle) whether this opportunity will lead to growth or depletion.

What did you decide? Is your opportunity one of growth or depletion?

When do I use my Decision Tree?

Because this is something new, I suggest starting out small and often. For example:

→ Say you would like to get a babysitter to take that yoga class on Thursday nights.

→ Or you want to hit the gym at lunch time, but aren't sure you can fit it in between meetings.

→ You are considering that job offer, but the job you have seems to be just fine.

→ Or you just got the job offer of your dreams!

→ You just aren't sure it would work out or if it's worth it.

When you completed the balancing act, did you notice how easy it can be to write down the benefits versus how difficult it can be to write down the sacrifices? It's because our brains like to operate with less work—and thinking about what you will have to sacrifice takes effort! It also takes effort to consider, I mean *truly* consider, the opportunity.

That's why I suggest writing your decisions out, at least for one or two weeks. It's great practice for your brain! And helpful on the emotional side, too. The more you do it, the easier the process becomes.

Your family Tree

By now you probably know the drill, but let's talk about how you can share this with your family. At this point, they may already be used to you sharing what you are learning from this book. And I have to admit that teaching others and helping them to use their own Decision Tree is not only fun, but something they will be able to use daily in their own lives.

If you recall, I recommended starting out small. For my kids, their Tree was related to extra-curricular activities. They love school, and they like to extend their school time with friends, which in our house means sports. If you were to come to our house on a random weekend, it would look like a sports supply store threw up on our lawn and cul-de-sac. Baseballs. Baseball bats. Hockey sticks. Lacrosse sticks. Soccer balls. Nets. You name it—I'm pretty sure we have it.

So when it comes to trying out for a team or joining one, we sit down with the boys and go through their own Decision Trees. Yes, they enjoy soccer and baseball and lacrosse, but they cannot play all three at once. We can play at home, but between the team practices, practicing at home, and games, that's not going to happen. At least, that's what is going on in my mind. Yet I do understand that they need to come to the decision on their own. So I walk them through the one-pager.

We did this recently because both of our boys love soccer and were given an opportunity to try out for both the town teams and a club team. One son said he wanted to stick with town immediately, but the other one wanted to think about it. He was excited about the opportunity! Playing more soccer would help his skill set–, and he loves the game. But when it came to thinking about what he would have to sacrifice, he realized it would result in practice four nights a week, plus games on weekends. It would also mean less day trips on the weekends, as well as sacrifices for the rest of the family in terms of the time and travel commitment.

In the end, it wasn't something he wanted to do. He said he would think about it next year, but it was a "no" for this year. As a parent, I would support whichever decision he made. If he wanted to play, we would find a way to make it happen, because it's important to him. But what was great about this exercise is that he started to realize that some decisions are not obvious. Some decisions require thought.

This is also an example of how even though my son doesn't necessarily have his three Guiding Words, this process is easy to understand.

→ There are only so many hours in the day.
→ There are only so many activities you can do.
→ You need to eat.
→ You need to sleep.
→ And you need some down time to just be *you*.

It doesn't always come down to sports, as there are many other opportunities, but a few clients shared scenarios they have experienced with their kids:

> What will it bring them if they play soccer and lacrosse?
> What will they have to give up?
> Is it worth it?

> What will it bring them if they do cub scouts and theater?
> What will they have to sacrifice?
> Is it worth it?

> What will it bring them to get a part-time job?
> What will they have to sacrifice?
> Is it worth it?

The scenarios are endless—and personal—but try taking them through the process. Before you know it, they will be making rational decisions based on their own Decision Trees!

Well, most of the time . . . .

We can help family members make decisions, but the ones that stick usually aren't those we make for them.

It can take time, and frankly, it's sometimes super frustrating! But just think about the power you are giving to your children when you sit down with them and talk them through their options, how they feel about them, what they like doing, and in the end, what they can reasonably do.

BONUS: When you sit with your child or your spouse and ask them the questions on the worksheet, it's not you asking—it's the worksheet!

Which brings me to the next balancing act . . . .

Balancing Act

> ### Your Family's Decision Tree
>
> Before you start this challenge, grab your journal or your downloadable workbook from your resources page: http://amysmalarz.com/book/
>
> The next time your spouse, partner or child comes to you with a decision they need to make, share your Decision Tree tool with them.
>
> Ask them the questions—or give them a copy to fill out themselves—and then come back together to talk about it.
>
> Despite the rolling of the eyes you may receive, the smile and confidence displayed after the process will make it all worth it!

All right. You are now the proud owner of your foundation and your support!

You have your:

→ Guiding Words

→ Action WOT

→ "Important" versus "urgent" definitions

→ Decision Tree

Just sit for a moment and admire all of the work you have put in so far. Amazing!
How does it feel?

→ Does it feel good?

→ Do you feel strong?

→ Do you feel grounded?

→ Do you feel like you can weather any storm?

You have now completed the first two phases of building your own Home. And
what's even better is that you are not only building your Home, but modeling it for
your loved ones, your family. Remember, we learn best by teaching others, and
others learn from us by seeing what we do.

There is just one more phase to completing the blueprint you can use to build your
Home. That's defining and shaping your protection.

Are you ready? Let's go!

Phase III:

Your Protection

"People protect what they love. What will you protect?" – Jacques Cousteau

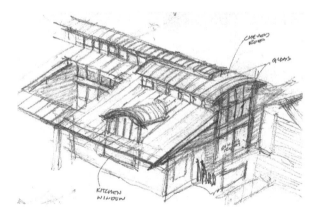

Chapter 9

What is Your Protection?

"People protect what they love. What will you protect?" – Jacques Cousteau

This quote by Jacques Cousteau speaks for itself. You have taken the time and energy to build your foundation and construct your two support systems: your "important" versus their "urgent" and your Decision Tree.

Now the key to keeping all of that safe is your protection. When you think about a roof for a home, it needs to be strong. If there are holes, the elements can get through. If it's too big, it will collapse in on the support walls and foundation. If it isn't big enough, well, there's no protection.

So now it's time to create your protection. Like the other phases you've already completed, some thought is required for the process. And the final pieces of the process is developing your own definition of Living Intentionally.

Your progress

In the beginning of the book, I mentioned that some of you would want to jump right in and create your definition of Living Intentionally. But it was important to wait. You needed to do the other work first, because now you are ready to think about, create and give shape to your definition of Living Intentionally.

You have taken the time to build the foundation and support for your Home, and now is the time to build the piece that will protect it and give it shape.

Your definition of Living Intentionally is not just words, not just a sentence. It reflects your foundation. It relates to your supporting structures, what holds your home in place. It is the final touch to the Home you are building for yourself.

But before we jump into creating your definition of Living Intentionally, let's take some time to remind your brain of all that you have accomplished up to this point. I want you to take a few minutes to capture, all in one place, the work and thought you have put in so far.

On to the next balancing act . . . .

Your Progress and Your Home

Before you start this challenge, grab your journal or your downloadable workbook from your resources page: http://amysmalarz.com/book/

Get your pen and journal and write down the following:

- Your three Guiding Words
- Your action WOT (for today or tomorrow)
- What does "important" mean to you?
- What was at least one "important" item on your list today?
- What type of growth opportunities have you accepted recently (today or this week)?

Now, take a moment to read what you just wrote. Amazing!

How does that make you feel?

→ Do you feel empowered?

→ Do you feel proud?

→ Do you feel as if you are making progress?

I, for one, am super excited for you. All of this takes time and dedication, so here's a big high-five to you for giving yourself the most precious gifts: time, love and respect. Working through this process has exposed more of that beautiful, smart and strong person inside that has always been there but is shining a bit more brightly now.

Now that you are grounded, let's move to the final phase!

Chapter 10

How do you define Living Intentionally?

"Don't make the mistake of believing that your future hangs on one big defining moment. Every moment is defining you whether you realize it or not."
– Kerri Weems

Now comes the final piece of your Home, your protection, the seal that protects your foundation and your support. You may be asking:

"How the heck do I define Living Intentionally?"

"Where do I start?"

While these are good questions, you already know the answer.

You start with **YOU**.

Remember: you've gone through the exercises to think of three words that describe your truest, best self, the person you want to be. You have daily action WOT that remind you to turn your intentions into actions. You have taken the initiative and started to include at least one "important" thing for you on your list each day. And you have given time and space for the emotional and logical parts of your brain to work together to make decisions.

All of that works toward this final piece: how you define to yourself and the world what Living Intentionally means to YOU.

But I can see you shaking your head, thinking, "Um, I still don't know where to start."

I get it. Sometimes it's hard to wrap your head around something like this, because while it's a necessary step, it can feel like a really big one.

The first thing you should do is take a deep breath, maybe even two. Just sit for a moment and let your mind wander to your Guiding Words and action WOT. Let your mind play with those words and notice the feeling you have inside of you. You may be at peace or excited.

One way to come up with your definition of Living Intentionally is to use your Guiding Words and maybe even an action WOT or two in a sentence. Not too long ago, I guided about fifty people through a 5 Day Living Intentionally Challenge. Here are some of their definitions of Living Intentionally:

> "When I say Living Intentionally, I think of being rooted to the earth, yet reaching out to the sky   to be all I can be."
>
> "Living Intentionally to me means agreeing with everything God says I am. Aligning my life, in active faith of thought, word and action."
>
> "When I think of Living Intentionally I think of being aware, grateful and living in my self-worth."

As you can see, these definitions are unique and personal. And what I learned during the challenge is each of these folks incorporated either their Guide Words or action WOT into their sentences.

For me, personally, my definition of Living Intentionally is:

> *"Everyone has a voice and deserves to be heard. Living Intentionally, for me, is helping others bring out their voice, and share it with others so they can communicate and be heard."*

Now, the trick here is to take this seriously, but don't think of it as a life-or-death situation. Don't think about whether it's perfect or wrong.

It won't be perfect.

It won't be wrong.

Earlier I referenced my podcast, "Living Intentionally with Amy Smalarz." One of the questions I ask each guest is:

"What does Living Intentionally mean to you?"

Such a simple yet powerful question. At the time of this writing, I have over sixty different definitions on hand. Here are just a few to give you an idea of the diversity and beauty of how others define Living Intentionally.

Aligning my life, in active faith of thought, word and action.

Being aware, grateful and living in my self-worth.

Getting into alignment with my core values.

Recognition of how I do one thing is how I do everything.

Being aware and having a purpose.

131

Being a master of my own destiny.

And let me say again, don't worry that your definition isn't perfect or that it's wrong...

It won't be perfect.

It won't be wrong.

The key here is to write something down from your heart and mind.

Your body is primed for this right now. You have just spent the past few minutes thinking about all of the work you have done and what you have given yourself to this point. There is no turning back now.

So, on to the next balancing act!

Your Progress and Your Home

Before you start this challenge, grab your journal or your downloadable workbook from your resources page: http://amysmalarz.com/book/

Your turn!

Taking all that you have done so far (I highly recommend looking back at your notes or at least reading your responses to the previous balancing act) and the examples of how others define Living Intentionally, write down YOUR definition of Living Intentionally.

NOTE: You will not be graded on this, and no one will see this unless you show them, so make it brilliant!

Make it fun.

Make it totally, completely, 100 percent reflective of YOU!

And there you have it! The final piece of your Home!

Bringing your Home to your family

Writing the title of this section seems a bit silly at first, but when I thought about it, it rings true. You have built a Home for yourself, and you have been going through the process to get to a life balance.

Notice I didn't say work-life balance, but **LIFE** balance.

In our lives, there is no separation of work, tasks, and the things we enjoy. It's all just life, and it's up to us to balance what we have in front of us each day.

Your Home is a place where you can balance every day.

You are already equipped with:

→ A solid foundation
→ Strong support
→ Reinforced protection

You have all that you need.

And when it comes to sharing that with others, like I have said before, it's leading by example. People will feel your balance, and they'll want what you have. Your sense of self and level of love and respect for yourself will shine, and your family will feel it.

I've said this before and I'll say it again: there is no magic bullet. It takes work, and it takes practice each and every day. The way to share this with your family is to share your practice with them every day.

In a previous chapter, I mentioned how we have a whiteboard in the kitchen.. I use it as a place to write down one of my action WOT each day. On Sundays, I write down one of my Guiding Words as well. By sharing my practice with my family, they are naturally curious.

I'm not sitting them down and having a family meeting on the importance of building your Home or defining your actions each day in a positive light. Can you imagine the reaction I would get? I am just being more of me. At the same time, I'm setting the example that what is most beautiful and cherished for each of us is being who we are and sharing that with others. And my boys see that every day.

I know that each family has their own ways of doing things and that a whiteboard may not work for you. But think of something that could work. Think of a way to bring and share your Home with your family.

You love them and want the best for them. Helping them to learn how they can be their truest, best selves and at the same time be loved and respected—that is one of the greatest gifts a parent can give to a child.

Which brings me to the last balancing act . . . .

Balancing Act

Your Family Share

Before you start this challenge, grab your journal or your downloadable workbook from your resources page: http://amysmalarz.com/book/

Earlier I asked you to come up with some family Guiding Words.

Take a moment and write those words down.

Now, as a family, come up with your own definition of how you can Live Intentionally each day, together.

You can write a sentence and keep that visible or do something like:

L = Love one another
O = Observe before judging
V = Value everyone
E = Empathy

You can use any word, but sometimes these are more fun! And the more fun they are, the more likely they are to stick...

Chapter 11

How do you maintain and build momentum?

> "You have brains in your head.
> You have feet in your shoes.
> You can steer yourself
> any direction you choose.
>
> And YOU are the guy who'll decide where to go.
>
> – Dr. Seuss (Oh, the Places You'll Go!)

While you are deciding where to go, or if you happen to get lost or sidetracked along the way, remember you are not alone. You have dedicated resources for you, for life, just from buying this book.

Practice, practice, practice.

It won't be perfect. What is "perfect," anyway? What matters is that you give yourself time to do this. And it's not just for you. While you are taking care of yourself first, you are also setting an example of how others around you can Live Intentionally.

There is also our private Facebook community that I highly encourage you to join. Yes, it's free, but more importantly it is filled with other awesome people like you who are on their own journey of building their Homes. I don't know about you, but I appreciate and enjoy being around like-minded people who want to be more of themselves and really contribute what they *know* they have inside.

Why would you not want that?

Last but not least, I would love for you to reach out to me directly at amy@amysmalarz.com.

Share your stories, ask questions, whatever. And I promise, if you ask a question and I don't know the answer, I will help you find on—or at least point you in the direction to get one.

You have opened yourself up just by reading this book. You see some of the possibilities, some of which you may never knew existed. You may have known options were there, but you didn't think you could attain them.

Now it's up to you to maintain your Home. That may mean some touch-ups, or it could be a whole re-model, but the key thing to remember is that it's yours.

You made it.

You live in it.

You share it with others.

And with that, I would like to congratulate you and leave you with one final quote.

Acknowledgements

I want to say thank you for being a part of the Living Intentionally movement. It is my mission to reach and serve a million people in the next two years to help them be their truest, best selves and show up how they want to be in the world. You are a part of that. If there is someone you know can benefit from being a part from this movement, do them a favor and buy them a copy of this book to share with them. They will be thankful and look to you as someone who care and loves them.

I cannot close this book without sharing some special thanks with those who have come into my life in varying stages; who have helped make me who I am today; and who continue to love and challenge me each and every day.

My boys: Matty, Benny and Davey. This book and my life as I know it would not be possible without you. I can be a total and complete pain in the ass, but I also love you with my whole heart and soul, and I am grateful each and every day that I have the opportunity to bug and love you! And most grateful that you put up with me and love me, too!

Mom and Dad. Not enough words to say what I really feel, but they are amazing. Loving, caring, supportive and just always there for me. Always.

My coaches and mentors: Jeff Moore, Alex Charfen, Adam Toren, Bo Eason, Nancy Turnbull, Alice Sapienza, Mr. Burbridge, Torch...Just to name a few. Tough acts to follow—which is why you have shown and told me to be my unique self. But it helps to learn from the best!

A special thanks to Katie Willson who goes above and beyond each and every day!

And to all my friends who have supported and put up with me as I write this book - THANK YOU! There are too many to name and knowing me, I would miss a few but please know that I could not have done this without you. This includes all of the awesome people in my groups, Intentional Living and Women's Biz Accelerator. Your participation, questions, insights are what keep me going each and every day!

About the Author

Amy is the creator of the proprietary framework Communicate To Be Heard™ as she believes that each of us has a voice that deserves to be heard. When you are a client working with Amy, she helps you to discover and define that voice or that value message and then helps you to translate that to other people so you can Communicate To Be Heard™. When that happens, you are truly able to live a life with greater intention.

Amy is also the host of the Podcast, Living Intentionally with Amy Smalarz: http://amysmalarz.com/living-intentionally-podcast/ and the founder of the Women's Biz Accelerator. : https://www.linkedin.com/groups/8478726

Amy lives by her 5 core concepts:

Learn
Produce more and better results.

Individualize
Know your unique traits and characteristics that distinguish you from everyone else.

Activate
Be energized by opportunities and possibilities; empower people.

Achieve
Identify problems and implement appropriate and unique solutions.

Compete
Be the champion! Fuel the desire to be the very best!

For many years she struggled with trying to live up to what she perceived as everyone else's expectations of her – as a woman, wife, mother and daughter – and in the process, she lost herself. So, now she dedicates her time and effort to help you accelerate your personal and professional growth.

She is the proud mama of the two lights of her life, her sons, Matty and Benny. She is also blessed to have not only found her soulmate and best friend, but knows she is fortunate enough that he has stuck around for 20 years! In her free time, she loves being outdoors, hanging out at the fire pit and coaching her son's community-ed basketball team.

She doesn't want you to survive.

She wants you to live intentionally. And she wants to show you how.

You can reach Amy at amy@amysmalarz.com or http://amysmalarz.com/